REFLECTIONS ON FAITH INSPIRED BY
MEN

Phil Ridden

EDWEST PUBLISHING

Copyright © Phil Ridden, 2020

Published 2020 by Edwest Publishing
Joondalup, Western Australia
www.edwestpublishing.biz

ISBN: Paperback 978-0-9925481-5-5

All rights reserved. No part of this publication may be reproduced or transmitted, in any form or by any means without the permission of the author, except for fair use in worship and study.

To contact the author:
Phil@philridden.com.au
www.philridden.com.au

CONTENTS

Dedication	iv
Why this book?	v
Why men?	vi
A word about Biblical quotes	vii
SHEPHERDS	1
BEING MALE	2
WATCHING SPORT	4
LISTENING	5
DRIVING	6
COMPETITION	8
HELL	10
HOPE	12
RISK	14
SMARTER	16
WORKING WITH MY HANDS	18
FAILED TO LOVE	20
HANDS	22
INDIVIDUAL	24
HONESTY	26
HUFFING AND PUFFING	28
LIKE JESUS	30
MATESHIP	32
SHAME	34
MOON	36
OPPONENT	38

MANHOOD	40
STEAK	42
A QUICK DRINK	44
ARGUMENT	46
SO FAR	48
PHONE	50
MISSED PROMOTION	51
PREJUDICE	52
ANGER	53
WORK	54
OLD HANDS	56
AGEING	58
TOOLS	60
MEDALS	62
THE GAME	63
MET SOMEONE	64
CHOOSING	66
FIDELITY	68
FAITH	69
FAILED TO COMMUNICATE	70
DOUBLE BED	72
LOVE THEIR MOTHER	74
HOLDING TIGHT	76
ASKING	77
JUMPING	78
ACROSS THE ROOM	80

A MAN LIKE ME	82
PRAM	84
PARENT	86
KISSES	87
MAN	88
FATHER FIGURE	90
MISSING HIM	92
INTERESTS	94
STARING	95
WITH YOU	96
HIS HERO	98
TIME	99
THANKS	100

Dedication

This book is dedicated to my family, and to the congregations who have challenged me to share my understanding of faith.

Why this book?

More than fifty years ago, Michel Quoist wrote:

> *If we knew how to listen to God, if we knew how to look around us, our whole life would become prayer. ... Words are only a means. However, the silent prayer which has moved beyond words must always spring from everyday life, for everyday life is the raw material of prayer.*[1]

If we seek God, we will see Him revealed in the people and events in our lives.

Including the experiences and emotions associated with being male. The things men do and say and think and feel can challenge us to think about faith; reveal God to us; and teach us about our relationship with our Eternal Father/Mother.

That is the purpose of this book. As you read these reflections, it is likely they will conjure familiar images for you. I hope they will also help you to meditate on God and your relationship with Him.

This is not a book to be read from cover to cover. It is designed to be dipped into, sequentially or not, with favourite passages revisited from time to time. Perhaps it will inspire you to add your own reflections on the theme.

---

[1] Michel Quoist, *Prayers of life,* MH Gill and Sons Ltd, Dublin, 1963, p. 22.

Why men?

This book is written primary for men—but not exclusively.

In recent years, we men have endured serious criticism, just for being male.

Some of it we have brought upon ourselves, because of stereotypically masculine behaviour. You will be familiar with the list of such behaviours.

We excuse too much, often with clichés like, 'Boys will be boys' and 'Men will be men' and 'Blame it on the testosterone'. But that it not who most men are. It is not who men need to be.

There is so much to celebrate about men. There are so many of us—men and women—who are grateful for the men who have influenced our lives.

This book accepts the characteristics and interests which are typical of many men, but turns them into reflections on faith. Hopefully, it will help you to reflect on the men who have blessed your life.

A word about Biblical quotes

A Biblical quote is included for each reflection—yet I do this with a little discomfort. It is too easy to extract verses from their context where they have a particular meaning, and to use them to convey another meaning in a different context. It is possible I have done that in this book—not to give credibility, but to help you to delve into the Bible and to seek out its truth. Forgive me if I've been simplistic. If the Biblical references are helpful, explore them; if not, ignore them.

Contemporary translations have been used. All are available (free of charge) online from various sites.

Bible Translations quoted:

Scripture quotations marked **NIV** are taken from *The Holy Bible: New International Version®*, NIV® Copyright © 1973, 1978, 1984, 2011 by Biblica, Inc.® Used by permission. All rights reserved worldwide.

Scripture quotations marked **GNT** are taken from *Good News Translation®* (Today's English Version, Second Edition), Copyright © 1992 American Bible Society. All rights reserved.

Scripture quotations marked **MSG** are taken from *The Message*. Copyright © 1993, 1994, 1995, 1996, 2000, 2001, 2002. Used by permission of NavPress Publishing Group.

Scripture quotations marked **TLB** are from *The Living Bible* copyright © 1971 by Tyndale House Foundation. Used by permission of Tyndale House Publishers Inc., Carol Stream, Illinois 60188. All rights reserved.

SHEPHERDS

I like that you chose shepherds, Father.

You wanted to announce the greatest birth ever,
The birth of your son.
So you arranged an outdoor concert,
With a full angel choir,
To entertain …
Shepherds!

Not the local government officials,
    religious leaders,
    community leaders,
    chamber of commerce.
No.
Shepherds.
    men who slept outdoors,
    wrestled wild animals,
    ate meat,
    and rarely washed.

Did you do that so that men—
Ordinary blokes—
Would realise this news was for us?

When the angels had left them and gone into heaven, the shepherds said to one another, 'Let's go to Bethlehem and see this thing that has happened, which the Lord has told us about.' (Luke 6: 15, NIV)

BEING MALE

I worry for my gender, Father.

For many generations,
In many cultures,
Man has dominated,
Suppressing women,
Depriving them of power and rights.

You saw it when you were on earth.
You spoke up for a woman caught in adultery,
    about to be punished by death,
    while the man was unnamed.
You told a story of a woman
    unable to get justice from a judge,
    because she was a woman.
You challenged men,
    who judged the morality of a woman,
    but were self-righteous about their own.

Our society has come so far in gender equity,
Yet we men have so far to go.
Statistics and stories declare our faults:
    violence against those we profess to love,
    binge drinking, alcoholism and drug addiction,
    predatory sexual behaviour,
    dangerous driving,

unfaithfulness and promiscuity,
neglect of financial and moral responsibility for children,
abuse of ourselves and others …
To prove our 'manhood' or
Declare our independence.

Jesus showed how to be a man—
Courageously standing for what is right;
Loving uncompromisingly;
Showing compassion,
    forgiveness,
        blessing;
Putting the needs of others before himself—
A strong and confident man's man,
Yet with a sensitive heart.

Will you help me to be a man,
Your way, Father?

So, chosen by God for this new life of love, dress in the wardrobe God picked out for you: compassion, kindness, humility, quiet strength, discipline. Be even-tempered, content with second place, quick to forgive and offence. Forgive as quickly and completely as the Master forgave you. And regardless of what else you put on, wear love. It's your basic, all-purpose garment. Never be without it. (Colossians 3: 12–14, MSG)

WATCHING SPORT

I love watching sport, Father.

For a short time,
I'm distracted
    from work,
    from chores,
    from responsibilities.
I lose myself in the game.

The kids have gone to their rooms.
My wife has gone to bed.
It's just me—and the TV.

How often do I lose myself in you, Father,
When it's just me—and you?

At that time Jesus went up a hill to pray and spent the whole night there praying to God. (Luke 6: 12, GNT)

LISTENING

I did it again, Father.
I talked too much
    and listened too little.
I was so concerned to ensure that everyone heard
    my point of view,
That I didn't give them a hearing.

Father,
I believe you often speak through people –
Sometimes you even speak through me!

Teach me to listen,
So that I may hear your voice
In the voices of others.

Run away from infantile indulgence. Run after mature righteousness—faith, love, peace—joining those who are in honest and serious prayer before God. Refuse to get involved in inane discussions; they always end up in fights. God's servant must not be argumentative, but a gentle listener and a teacher who keeps cool, working firmly but patiently with those who refuse to obey. (2 Timothy 2: 22–23, MSG)

DRIVING

I love cars, Father.

The smells:
    petrol fumes,
    hot engine,
    burning tyres.
The sounds:
    straining engine,
    clunking gears,
    squealing tyres.
The power:
    G-force against my chest,
    seat pressing into my back,
    the wheel dragging against my hands.

And I love going fast, Father.
I'm not normally reckless;
I'm not normally a law-breaker;
I'm not normally an idiot behind the wheel.
But I love to go fast,
    especially on twisting
    or unsurfaced roads.
There is an adrenaline rush
    in pushing the limits;
Feeling the forces of momentum
    on my body,
    on my car.
I think you understand, Father.

Thousands of years ago,
You had a servant, Jehu,
    who loved his chariot,
    and was known for his fast driving.
The lookout who saw him coming said:
'The driving is like that of Jehu son of Nimshi—
    he drives like a maniac.'[2]
I think I'd have liked Jehu,
Although we might not have been good for each other.

Father, you gave me these feelings,
Not to cause destruction
    to myself or others,
But to help me to protect myself,
And to equip me to deal with crises.

Remind me, Father, to slow down,
    to enjoy the world I pass,
    to cause less stress to others,
    to allow space in my thoughts—
For you.

Slow down. Take a deep breath. What's the hurry? Why wear yourself out? Just what are you after anyway? But you say, 'I can't help it. I'm addicted to alien gods. I can't quit.' (Jeremiah 2: 25, MSG)

---

[2] 2 Kings 9: 20

COMPETITION

I'm competitive, Father.

I play sport, even table games, to win.
I want my favourite team to win.
I want to be first in the queue.
I want to be first away from the traffic lights.
I want to be the best at work.
I wanted to get top scores at school.

Why am I like this, Father?
It's the testosterone, people say;
It's a man thing.
But not all men are like this:
    not all are visibly competitive,
    not all are aggressive in their desire to win.

Am I insecure?
Am I trying to prove something
    to others
    or to myself?

Father, your acceptance of me is unconditional.
Your love for me is assured.
Grant me the peace of knowing
That there is nothing I need do
To prove my worth
To you.

My child, when the LORD corrects you, pay close attention and take it as a warning. The LORD corrects those he loves, as parents correct a child of whom they are proud. (Proverbs 3: 11–12, GNT)

HELL

It's hell without you, Father.

I've been there.
Of course I doubt sometimes,
    but I allowed doubt to win over belief.
Of course I question sometimes,
    but I allowed questions to win over answers.
Of course I find it difficult to trust sometimes,
    but I allowed uncertainty to win over trust.

And when I allowed myself to drift,
I was alone—
Without purpose,
    or passion,
    or reason …
And it was hell.

Is that what hell is, Father—
The absence of you?

Don't let me wander, Father.
Don't let me drift.
Don't let me find myself alone,
    without you.

Let me know the intimate companionship
Of your Spirit,
Within me—
Always …
Always …
Always …

When things were going great I crowed, 'I've got it made. I'm GOD's favourite. He made me king of the mountain.' Then you looked the other way and I fell to pieces. (Psalm 30: 6–7, MSG)

HOPE

What happened to hope, Father?

Every generation has its troubles:
Nuclear war,
Environmental catastrophe,
Economic disaster,
Social chaos,
Cancer and other health monsters,
Unemployment,
Homelessness and displacement,
Terrorism …

The focus shifts;
The uncertainty and apprehension doesn't.

I worry for our youth.
Where is their hope?
We hear their protests,
But what are protests without hope,
And their song of hope is muted.

The future should be better for each generation.
If we do our parenting right, our children will have
    the knowledge,
    the ability,
    the will,
    the morality,
    and the faith

To lead the world into a future filled with hope—
    hopefully.

Other religions require achievements,
    scores,
    payment,
To give them any hope of a better future.
In Jesus, you have already paid the price.
You ask nothing,
Except faith,
And in return you give hope—
Hope that you wait every day to lead us;
Hope that you wait at the end of life to welcome us.

Do my words give meaning to that hope?
Does my life give substance to that hope?

Lead me; teach me; for you are the God who gives me salvation. I have no hope except in you. (Psalm 25: 5, TLB)

RISK

We men are risk takers, Father.

There are jokes about men's famous last words:
    Let's see how fast she can go.
    They couldn't hit an elephant from that dist ...
    It's all right, the gun isn't loaded.
    Of course I know a mushroom from a toadstool.
    I always take this short cut across the railway
    lines.

There are frequent stories about it in the news:
    The vehicle was travelling at 130 in a 60 zone.
    The boys had been binge drinking for four hours.
    The youth was walking along the ledge at the top
    of the building when he fell.

We men are risk takers,
But often for wrong reasons.

I'd like to risk for you, Father,
To make myself vulnerable
    in sharing my experience of you,
    in stepping out in faith,
    in speaking for you,
    in expressing your love,
    in owning my beliefs,
    in sharing doubt as well as assurance,
    in avoiding clichés to dismiss difficult questions.

Am I a risk-taker, Father—
In faith?

Passing along, Jesus saw a man at his work collecting taxes. His name was Matthew. Jesus said, 'Come along with me.' Matthew stood up and followed him. (Matthew 9: 9, MSG)

SMARTER

I wish I was smarter, Father.

I used to think Dads were smarter than their children,
But now I'm a Dad I know I'm not.
I don't always know the answers to their questions;
I don't always know how to advise them;
I don't always know why things happen.

Children see through glib answers—
Simple answers to complex questions;
Cliché answers to meaningful questions;
Plagiarised answers to personal questions.

We could joke that
If Dads were smarter than their children,
Then Einstein's Dad would have been the one
    to develop the theory of relativity.
But more importantly,
If Dads were smarter than their children,
They would know the pain they cause
    when they walk out on the family.
If Dads were smarter than their children,
They would see how their drinking
    harms their children.
If Dads were smarter than their children,
They would understand their influence on their children
    and try to live as good men.

Like most men,
I'm not smarter than my children,
But I am more experienced with life,
    more experienced in assessing situations,
    more experienced in making decisions,
    more experienced in anticipating consequences,
    more experienced in trusting you.

I need your help, Father,
To share my experience
    wisely,
To share my wonder
    excitedly,
To share my expectations,
    graciously,
To share my uncertainty,
    sensitively,
To share my faith,
    Confidently.

I set plainspoken wisdom before you, my heart-seasoned understandings of life. I fine-tuned my ear to the sayings of the wise, I solve life's riddle with the help of a harp. (Psalm 49: 3–4, MSG)

WORKING WITH MY HANDS

I love to work with my hands, Father.

Most of my daily work is intellectual.
It requires me to think
    and articulate
    and write
    and plan
    and evaluate
    and reason
    and persuade …

But on the weekends, I work with my hands:
    maintaining the house,
    repairing the car,
    digging the garden,
    building a cubby,
    constructing furniture,
    renovating a vintage car,
    painting the house,
    repairing toys.
I love the sense of creating,
    achieving,
    completing,
    producing.

You understand, don't you, Father?
You were a carpenter,
A tradie.

You worked with your hands,
Creating and repairing.

You gave me these hands, Father.
Am I using them right?
Am I using them to serve you?

You yourselves know that these hands of mine have supplied my own needs and the needs of my companions. In everything I did, I showed you that by this kind of hard work we must help the weak, remembering the words the Lord Jesus himself said: 'It is more blessed to give than to receive.' (Acts 20: 34–35, NIV)

FAILED TO LOVE

I failed to love, Father,
    the way you love.

He irritated me.
The words he spoke,
    his manner,
    his appearance,
    his very presence,
    irritated me—angered me.
I couldn't wait to get away from him.

I could list the myriad things about him
That he should correct
    if he wants to get on with people.
I can't think of one good thing to say about him.

Forgive me, Father.
We are conditioned by this world to love people
    if they lovable,
    if they care about us,
    if they are kind to us,
    if they do things for us,
    if they …
Our love is selfish,
Seeking the best for ourselves.

You taught us to love people
    in spite of …
He may not be my sort of person,
He may not like me,
He may have traits that irritate me,
He may be unlikeable,
But he is your child.

Help me to love him
As you love me—
In spite of all that *I* am!

You're familiar with the old written law, 'Love your friend,' and its unwritten companion, 'Hate your enemy.' I'm challenging that. I'm telling you to love your enemies. Let them bring out the best in you, not the worst. When someone gives you a hard time, respond with the energies of prayer, for then you are working out of your true selves, your God-created selves. (Matthew 5: 43-45, MSG)

HANDS

My hands are expressive, Father.

A single gesture can signify so much:
    a fist,
    an open hand,
    a pointing finger,
    a clap,
    a handshake,
    a pat on the shoulder,
    a slap …

Hands are so expressive:
    reaching out or pushing away,
    caressing or hitting,
    holding or rejecting.

But when I pray
I fold them together,
    and all the actions of rejection and acceptance,
    all the words of insensitivity and compassion,
    all the feelings of pain and joy,
    all the past memories and future hopes,
All come together
When I fold my hands and pray.

Father, forgive me for who I ought not to have been;
Accept me for who I am;
And lead me to who I can be.

Stay alert; be in prayer so you don't wander into temptation without even knowing you're in danger. There is a part of you that is eager, ready for anything in God. But there's another part that's as lazy as an old dog sleeping by the fire. (Matthew 26: 41, MSG)

INDIVIDUAL

With you, I'm just me, Father.

We humans
    group people,
    categorise them,
    label them,
    define them,
And then judge them according to our own stereotyping.
We make judgements according to
    appearance,
    or voice,
    or manner,
    or history,
    or vocation,
    or possibilities,
    or the views of friends …

But you don't deal in prejudice.
With you, I am me.
No-one else.
Just who I am—
With my baggage,
    my worries,
    my weaknesses,
    my failures,
    my insecurities,
    my inadequacies …

And with my God-given skills,
    my passions,
    my strengths,
    my hopes,
    my dreams,
    my ambitions …

I love that about you, Father.
You made each of us
    unique,
    gifted,
    equipped to serve you.
All we have to do is hear your call,
And be ready to follow
Wherever,
Whenever,
You lead us.

Have I heard, Father?
Am I ready?
Am I following?

Anyone who intends to come with me has to let me lead. You're not in the driver's seat—I am. Don't run from suffering; embrace it. Follow me and I'll show you how. Self-help is no help at all. Self-sacrifice is the way, my way, to finding yourself, your true self. (Luke 9: 23, MSG)

HONESTY

I want to be honest with you, Father.

I'd like to say that I understand everything in the Bible.
    I don't.
I'd like to say that I trust you implicitly.
    I don't.
I'd like to say that I have answers to all of people's questions about faith.
    I don't.
I'd like to be able to explain why good people suffer and bad people thrive.
    I can't.
I'd like to say I will always live as you expect.
    I won't.
I'd like to say that I never have any doubt.
    I can't.
I'd like to say that I agree with everything the Bible says about how to live.
    I don't.

But, Father, I'm on the journey.
I'd like to say I genuinely want to live your way.
    I can—at least, most of the time.
I'd like to say I earnestly want to serve you.
    I can—at least, most of the time.
I'd like to say that I trust in your grace.
    I can—at least, most of the time.

I'd like to say that I know you love me,
    even when I fail,
    or I'm confused,
    or I'm distracted,
    or I struggle with doubt.
And I can—at least most of the time.

On this journey of faith—
This adventure—
Am I learning?
Am I growing?
Am I maturing?

In one way or another, God makes sure that we all experience what it means to be outside so that he can personally open the door and welcome us back in. (Romans 11: 32, MSG)

HUFFING AND PUFFING

I think I over-reacted, Father.

It was just a minor issue:
A parcel was coming,
So I asked for a phone call to indicate when,
    but that was apparently too difficult.
So I waited—
    all day—
    until I had to go out.
I was gone fifteen minutes,
But that was the moment the delivery arrived;
And because I wasn't home,
    it was returned to the post office—
Not my local post office,
But a distant one.
So began a long trip through pre-Christmas traffic,
    and a long wait in a long line.

I was not happy!
Such incompetence!
I said so
    to the post office representative
    who eventually found my parcel.
How hard would it have been
    to let me know a delivery time?
'We don't do that, sir.'
Well perhaps you should.

And why this post office?
'I don't know, sir.
It must have been an error.
I'm sorry.
Can I help you with anything else today, sir?'

It was frustrating,
    annoying,
    embarrassing,
    humbling.
I'm the Christian.
I'm the one who tries to follow Christ's example.
I'm the one who tries to live as Jesus would.
Yet she was the one who showed grace.
Her day was surely long,
    and busy,
    and stressful;
But she smiled and apologised.
And I …
    I did not.

Forgive me, Father.
I'll try to do better next time, Father.
Be patient.

Post this at all the intersections, dear friends: Lead with your ears, follow up with your tongue, and let anger straggle along in the rear. God's righteousness doesn't grow from human anger. (James 1: 19–21, MSG)

LIKE JESUS

I am awed by Jesus, Father.

In Sunday School I learnt about
    'Gentle Jesus, meek and mild'.
That's not the Jesus I read about or know.

He confronted the religious leaders,
    men with power over his life,
And called them hypocrites.
When a crowd confronted him angrily,
    moved to throw him off a cliff,
He stared them down and walked through them.
When he had the chance to be a celebrity,
    entertained by the wealthy,
He used the opportunity to point out their failings.
When men used the temple as a marketplace,
    exploiting and defrauding people,
He brandished a whip and drove them all out.
When given the opportunity
    to impress the Roman Governor with his innocence,
He kept silent.
When he had the power
    to free himself from the cross,
He endured the pain and humiliation.

This was no weakling.

This was a man.

I'm not sure how strong a man I am,
But I'm trying, Father:
Trying to stand up for what's right;
Trying to speak out against wrong;
Trying to walk beside the vulnerable;
Trying to challenge evil;
Trying to question society's values, goals, assumptions,
    where they conflict with yours;
Trying to tell of your love;
Trying to model your love.

Am I yet a man, Father—
    your man?

There isn't enough time for me to speak of Gideon, Barak, Samson, Jephthah, David, Samuel, and the prophets. Through faith they fought whole countries and won. They did what was right and received what God had promised. They shut the mouths of lions, put out fierce fires, escaped being killed by the sword. They were weak, but became strong; they were mighty in battle and defeated the armies of foreigners. ... Others, refusing to accept freedom, died under torture in order to be raised to a better life. (Hebrews 11: 32–35, GNT).

MATESHIP

Why do men pressure me to conform, Father?

I'm all for friendship,
    mateship,
    companionship
Among men.
I think it's healthy for men to share
    fishing,
    coffee,
    sports,
    concerns,
    stresses …
With other men.

But why do they deny others their individuality?
Why expect them to conform?
These men,
    who claim their independence,
    who contend that they are individuals,
    who are proud of their uniqueness,
Expect others to fit,
    to be part of the pack,
    to do as their peers do.

So they drink too much
    together.
They fight
    together.

They indulge in explicit sexual jokes
 together.
They use obscene language
 together.
Together,
 they bring out the worst in each other.

What can I do
 to bring out the best in other men?
What can I do
 to bring out the best in my son?
What can I do, Father,
 to be a worthy child to you?

Do not conform yourselves to the standards of this world, but let God transform you inwardly by a complete change of your mind. Then you will be able to know the will of God— what is good and is pleasing to him and is perfect. (Romans 12: 2, GNT)

SHAME

We men feel shame, Father.

We feel it when we drink too much,
When the habit of alcohol
Over-rides our common sense.

We feel it when we resort to violence,
Yelling, abuse, intimidation,
As a way of dealing with problems.

We feel it when we are absent fathers,
When our children
Are left to fend for themselves.

We feel it when we are unemployed,
When we are unable to provide
For our families.

We feel it when a seductive smile,
Or a shapely body,
Distracts us from our focus.

We feel it when we speak thoughtlessly,
Causing hurt or embarrassment
To those who deserve our respect.

We feel it when we allow sex
To lead us into behaviours and relationships
Which hurt others and ourselves.

We feel it when we cannot connect,
When our shyness
Prevents us from relating to others.

We blame testosterone for controlling us.
We blame expectations for pressuring us.
We blame others for provoking us.

How can I be a man, Father,
Who does not blame
And does not feel shame?

But Lord, you are my shield, my glory, and my only hope. You alone can lift my head, now bowed in shame. (Psalm 3: 3, TLB)

MOON

We looked at the moon together, Father.

It shone so brightly.
Silver paint glistened on
    leaves in the tree,
    the edge of a branch,
    windows,
    gutters,
    cars.
It lay a streamer of light across the water,
    shimmering,
    shining.
'How beautiful is the moon,' we said.

No it's not!
Humans have been there.
They have walked its surface,
And brought back samples of rocks and dust.
We have seen that
    it is not beautiful.
It is dusty and grey,
With not a colourful plant,
    nor a moving creature,
    to break the monotony.
It is pock-marked with craters,
Craters within craters,
Blasted by meteors crashing to the surface.
It is not beautiful in its own right.

The glowing beauty in which we delight
    is reflected light—
The glorious brilliance of the sun;
So bright that it is able to reflect beauty
    from a dull, grey surface.

We say, how beautiful is the moon.
We should say,
How beautiful is the sun;
How amazing in its brilliance,
That it can make a dull moon
    shine in beauty.

Father, I am a moon.
Of myself, I am dull,
A thing of no great attraction.
Yet when I reflect your light,
    your love,
    your glory,
I like to think that I shine.

Do I reflect your light?
Do I shine for you?

So watch out that the sunshine isn't blotted out. If you are filled with light within, with no dark corners, then your face will be radiant too, as though a floodlight is beamed upon you. (Luke 11: 35–36, TLB)

OPPONENT

I want to hurt him, Father.

He came straight at me—
Cannoned into me recklessly,
    as I was trying to retrieve the ball.
Now I'm on the sideline
    with a bleeding nose and sore ribs.
It could have been a broken neck.
It could have been concussion.
I'm convinced that was his purpose:
To get me off the field
    for the remainder of the game,
Because I was playing well—
Too well!
I want to get out there again—
    to target him,
    to take revenge,
    to send *him* to the sideline—
Preferably for the remainder of the season!

'Vengeance is mine'.
I know, Father, but …
Did you have to remind me of that?
'Love your enemy'.
That too, Father?
'Do good to those who hate you.'
I get it, Father.
I hear you.

When I get back out there,
Perhaps I will find him
    and shake his hand.
Perhaps I'll say,
'I don't know why,
    but God loves you, man,
    and says I have to too.'
Perhaps.

You showed me, Father,
    a new way to be,
    a new way to relate.
Help me, Father,
    to live it.

Since, then, we do not have the excuse of ignorance, everything—and I do mean everything—connected with that old way of life has to go. It's rotten through and through. Get rid of it! And then take on an entirely new way of life— a God-fashioned life, a life renewed from the inside and working itself into your conduct as God accurately reproduces his character in you. (Ephesians 4: 21–24, MSG)

MANHOOD

I'm confused about manhood, Father.

I want to be strong
For my wife and my children,
To be their protector,
    their wisdom,
    their strength.

But in so doing,
I am sometimes patronising,
    implying that others are incapable;
I am sometimes arrogant,
    implying that I know best;
I am sometimes dismissive,
    implying that my responsibility
        is beyond their comprehension.

Am I like that with you Father?
Do I sometimes imply
    that I don't need your help,
    that I know better than you,
    that you do not comprehend my responsibilities?

Forgive me, Father.
You are Creator,

The source of all strength,
    all knowledge,
    all wisdom.
And I yield my all to you.

Do you want to be counted wise, to build a reputation for wisdom? Here's what you do: Live well, live wisely, live humbly. It's the way you live, not the way you talk, that counts. (James 3: 13, MSG)

STEAK

I love a steak, Father.

It's man's food, I joke,
Meat—
Preferably a little rare,
The juices running across the plate
And down my chin.

It's clichéd, isn't it?
Meat doesn't make a man,
But it tastes good,
It feels good.

Am I a man when it comes to faith?
One of your men wrote about this,
Warning that,
When it came to faith,
Some of your followers were like children,
Still needing milk,
    when they should have been eating meat;
Still needing to be fed basics,
    when they should have been growing,
    maturing in the faith,
    knowledgeable,
    discerning,
    hanging in there even when things were tough.

When it comes to faith,
I want to be a man, Father,
Able to handle meat—
Able to understand your ways;
Able to discern your call;
Able to endure whatever the journey demands.

By this time you ought to be teachers yourselves, yet here I find you need someone to sit down with you and go over the basics on God again, starting from square one—baby's milk, when you should have been on solid food long ago! Milk is for beginners, inexperienced in God's ways; solid food is for the mature, who have some practice in telling right from wrong. (Hebrews 5: 12–14, MSG)

A QUICK DRINK

I worry about alcohol, Father.

It is everywhere,
Ubiquitously permeating
    our social events,
    our relationships,
    our advertising,
    our celebrations,
    our melancholy,
    our moments of reflection.

And the consequences are frightening:
    violence,
    road trauma,
    crime,
    destruction of property,
    damage to relationships,
    ill health ...
Outcomes we try to ignore
    or cover up.

Why do people need alcohol, Father,
    to lubricate their social interactions,
    to bolster their courage,
    and to be 'one of the boys'?

You are sufficient, Father—
Your Fatherly love;
Your grace, shown in Jesus;
Your companionship, known through your Spirit.
What other enabler do I need?

So whether you eat or drink or whatever you do, do it all for the glory of God. Do not cause anyone to stumble, whether Jews, Greeks or the church of God—even as I try to please everyone in every way. For I am not seeking my own good but the good of many, so that they may be saved. (1 Corinthians 10: 31–33, NIV)

ARGUMENT

I tried logic, Father, but I failed.

I wanted to convince him about the Gospel—
The good news
    of your love for humankind;
The story
    of Christ's life and claims and death and
    resurrection;
And the promise
    of the relationship we can have with you.

I reasoned;
Used logical argument;
Quoted Scripture;
Analysed his responses;
Pointed out his erroneous thinking;
Rebutted his arguments …

And it was wrong.
Because the Gospel defies logic.
It is beyond human reasoning—
That the Creator of the universe would
    come to earth,
    live as a man,
    allow himself to be ill-treated and killed;
Just to show how much he loves us—
    loves me.

Love defies logic—
Your love defies logic—
And I'm glad, Father.

Next time, Father,
Will you help me
To avoid argument and debate
And simply help him to see Jesus?

God didn't send me out to collect a following for myself, but to preach the Message of what he has done, collecting a following for him. And he didn't send me to do it with a lot of fancy rhetoric of my own, lest the powerful action at the centre—Christ on the Cross—be trivialized into mere words. (1 Corinthians 1: 17, MSG)

SO FAR

My Dad had a favourite psalm, Father.

It was Psalm 103.
You know it, of course.
> Praise the LORD, my soul!
> All my being, praise his holy name!
> Praise the LORD, my soul,
> and do not forget how kind he is.
> He forgives all my sins
> and heals all my diseases.
> He keeps me from the grave
> and blesses me with love and mercy.
> He fills my life with good things,
> so that I stay young and strong like an eagle.[3]

I like the sentiment, Father,
I like the vibe,
But it's not really true.

You don't heal all our diseases:
> people die from illness.
You don't keep us from the grave:
> we all die sooner or later.
We don't stay young and strong like an eagle:
> as we age, we weaken.

---

[3] Psalm 103: 1–5, GNT

But I understand what David was singing:
So far,
> you have been good to him,
> you have kept him safe and strong,
> you have forgiven his failings and sins,
> you have been patient with his weaknesses—

And so he overflows with gratitude.
And because of this, he is confident that
> you will continue to care for him.

Do I worry too much, Father?
Do I sometimes forget to be grateful
> for all your goodness?

Do I sometimes forget to be confident
> that you will continue with me?

The LORD is merciful and loving, slow to become angry and full of constant love. (Psalm 103: 8, GNT)

PHONE

I love modern phones, Father.

I have continual access to others,
> to speak to them,
> or to hear from them.

No matter where I am in the world,
> I am never out of contact,
> never isolated.

At any time, day or night,
> I can be in touch with those I love.

You invented the phone, Father.
I have continual access to you,
> to speak to you,
> or to hear from you.

No matter where I am in the world,
> I am never out of contact,
> never isolated.

At any time, day or night,
> I can be in touch with you.

Hello, Father …

Hear my cry, O God; listen to my prayer! In despair and far from home I call to you! (Psalm 61:1, GNT)

MISSED PROMOTION

What happened to my promotion, Father?

I thought I had put in the hard yards;
I thought I had played the politics;
I thought the boss was impressed;
I thought I was a shoo-in.
But no,
Someone else leap-frogged over me—
    young,
    female,
    been here for just six months!

I could scream discrimination,
    favouritism,
    unfair,
But she must have something I don't.
I shouldn't resent her age or her gender;
I shouldn't resent her skills;
I shouldn't resent the gifts she has.

But what about me?
Where do I go now?
What is my future now?

You, LORD, are all I have, and you give me all I need; my future is in your hands. (Psalm 16: 5, GNT)

PREJUDICE

I was prejudiced, Father.

I saw the tattoos on his arms and neck,
    his large frame,
    muscles bulging from the singlet,
    the careless attire …
And I was wary.
I assumed him to be a man to be avoided,
Lacking in respect or care for others.

And then he smiled,
    opened the door for me,
    and followed me into the shop.

You dined with collaborators;
You defended an accused prostitute;
You gathered restless children about you.

Do I judge too easily, Father?

You will be doing the right thing if you obey the law of the Kingdom, which is found in the scripture, 'Love your neighbour as you love yourself.' But if you treat people according to their outward appearance, you are guilty of sin, and the Law condemns you as a lawbreaker. (James 2: 8–9, GNT)

ANGER

I'm feeling angry, Father.

I am offended,
    affronted,
    and unable to do anything about it.
All I can do is to get angry.

Why did you give us anger?
It is such a pointless emotion.
It has no outlet
    except aggression.
I can yell;
I can swear;
I can hit someone or something;
I can throw something;
But none of that solves anything,
And it doesn't take away the anger.

But you can,
And I can learn to let you.

Go ahead and be angry. You do well to be angry—but don't use your anger as fuel for revenge. And don't stay angry. Don't go to bed angry. Don't give the Devil that kind of foothold in your life. (Ephesians 4: 26–27, MSG)

WORK

Thank you for work, Father.

I enjoy the sense of worth,
The feeling that I am doing something that matters.
We can all experience it:
> installing pipes, to provide water and sanitation,
> connecting cables, to provide power,
> selling furniture to make life comfortable,
> managing a business, to provide employment,
> teaching, to shape futures,
> healing, to make people well,
> fire-fighting, to save lives and property,
> mending roads, to enable safe travel,
> building houses, to provide shelter and comfort,
> growing food, to feed the world …

When we make a difference to people's lives,
> our work has worth.

Even working at home:
> repairing the car,
> building a barbecue,
> cleaning the pool,
> painting a wall,
> fixing a door,
> pulling weeds,
> mowing the lawn,
> vacuuming the floor,
> washing clothes,

repairing a toy,
cooking meals …
When we make a difference for our family
our work has worth.

You provide purpose, Father.
When we see what we do as serving you,
Then everything has worth.

I appeal to you to be shepherds of the flock that God gave you and to take care of it willingly, as God wants you to, and not unwillingly. Do your work, not for mere pay, but from a real desire to serve. Do not try to rule over those who have been put in your care, but be examples to the flock. (1 Peter 5: 2–3, GNT)

OLD HANDS

His hands have lived, Father.

I look at them as I hold them,
These ageing hands:
- wrinkled,
- criss-crossed by lines,
- distorted by arthritic bumps,
- scarred by numerous altercations with tools,
- skin rough and dry,
- nails ridged and uneven,
- blood vessels on the back a maze of pipelines.

These hands have lived.

But there is beauty in these hands:
- gentleness,
- softness,
- warmth,
- energy,
- playfulness.

These are hands that have loved and helped others.
These are hands that have served you.

Your hands were scarred by love for us—
    for me.
Thank you, Father.
Take my hands and use them in your service.

May your deeds be shown to your servants, your splendour to their children. May the favour of the Lord our God rest on us; establish the work of our hands for us — yes, establish the work of our hands. (Psalm 90: 16–17, NIV)

AGEING

They're ageing, Father.

I look at my parents
And see their years piling on top of one another
    in their faces,
    in their posture,
    in their movement.

I've seen the family photos:
Images of young people
    marrying,
    smiling,
    holding infants,
    embracing children
        at picnics,
        parties,
        family celebrations.

The light is still in their eyes.
The love is still in their expressions.
The mischief still tickles their smile.

And Father, like their love for me,
Their love for you continues—
    perhaps grows—
Because of their experiences,
    their insights,
    their years.

Life's trials have not dulled their faith,
> but polished it—
And it still shines.

Lead them into the future, Father.
Lead them into times and places
> where they may tell your story,
> where they may show your grace,
> where they may bring your love.

I'm ageing too, Father.
Is my faith still shining?
Is it being polished by my experiences of life
> and of you?

The righteous will flourish like palm trees; they will grow like the cedars of Lebanon. They are like trees planted in the house of the LORD, that flourish in the Temple of our God, that still bear fruit in old age and are always green and strong. (Psalm 92: 11–14, GNT)

TOOLS

I was looking through Dad's tools, Father.

When he died, they came to me:
    hand saws,
    hand drill,
    plane,
    spoke-shave,
    brace and bit,
    marking gauge,
    axe,
    assorted garden tools…

There are other tools mingled with my own tools:
    screwdrivers,
    chisels,
    spanners,
    wrenches …
    and assorted screws, bolts, nails and other fixings.

Some of the tools I regularly use,
Others rarely,
Some never.

But as I look at them,
I recall him using them,
Teaching me to use them.

He left me other tools, too—
Tools for life:
    values,
    attitudes,
    strategies for thinking and deciding and acting.
And faith.
He taught me about you.
He gave me a Bible.

Thank you, Father, for all he left me.
Help me to leave my kids with the right tools too.
Make me a tool in your hands
And use me to get jobs done for your kingdom.

Do not let any part of your bodies become tools of wickedness, to be used for sinning; but give yourselves completely to God—every part of you—for you are back from death and you want to be tools in the hands of God, to be used for his good purposes. (Romans 6: 13, TLB)

MEDALS

He wears his medals proudly, Father.

This old man,
Marching with pride,
Celebrating his role as a young man
In a conflict not of his making.

He doesn't celebrate war.
He never tells stories of war.
He fears that war might envelop his grandchildren.
No. What he remembers with his friends—
    remembers with pride—
Is their service:
    their willingness to face hardships,
    to risk their lives,
    in their country's service.

I serve you, Father.
But am I willing
    to face hardships,
    to risk my life
    in your service?

What does the LORD YOUR GOD ask of you but to fear the LORD your God, to walk in obedience to him, to love him, to serve the LORD your God with all your heart and with all your soul, and to observe the LORD's commands and decrees that I am giving you today for your own good? (Deuteronomy 10: 12–13, NIV)

THE GAME

I watched the game, Father.

What a debacle.
At no point did my team look like winning.
They almost set a team record
    for their worst defeat!
Now I feel frustrated,
    disappointed,
    irritated,
Over a game!

It's appalling, Father,
That a game—
    with no consequence for the spectators—
Should so affect our emotions,
That we feel a need to express it
In inappropriate ways.

Help me, Father, to maintain a right perspective.

*So if you're serious about living this new resurrection life with Christ, act like it. Pursue the things over which Christ presides. Don't shuffle along, eyes to the ground, absorbed with the things right in front of you. Look up, and be alert to what is going on around Christ—that's where the action is. See things from **his** perspective. (Colossians 3: 1–2, MSG)*

MET SOMEONE

I've met someone, Father,

I can't get her out of my mind.
I'm in awe of her beauty:
    the attraction of her smile,
    the knowing depth in her eyes,
    the smell of her perfume,
    the flow of her hair,
    the shape of her body.

How do I tell, Father,
If this is infatuation or love?
How do I know if she is right for me—
If she will make me a better man
    than I could have hoped to be?
How can I know if I am right for her—
If my love will help her to be
    all that you created her to be?

As in anything, Father,
I go forward in trust:
If this is right for us,
Then go ahead of us,
Leading us to a shared future,
A shared faith,
A shared love.

There are four things that are too mysterious for me to understand: an eagle flying in the sky, a snake moving on a rock, a ship finding its way over the sea, and a man and a woman falling in love. (Proverbs 30: 18–19, GNT)

CHOOSING

You can't choose who you fall in love with, Father.

That's what society says.
So leave your wife,
    your children,
    your life,
And yield to your passions.

It's so superficial,
    so naïve.
We may not choose who we fall in love with,
But we can choose what we do about it.

It is selfish to yield to our passions
    when others get hurt.
It is wrong to yield to our passions
    when it ignores your law of love.

Yet it is easy to be seduced
    by the dominant values,
    by the accepted activities,
    by the prevalent attitudes,
    by the ubiquitous prejudices,
    by the popular ideas,
Which surround me every day.

Father, will you guide me
When I am tempted
   by values,
   by activities,
   by attitudes,
   by prejudices,
   by ideas,
Which society promotes,
And which seem attractive,
But which ignore your law of love?

Avoid the passions of youth, and strive for righteousness, faith, love, and peace, together with those who with a pure heart call out to the Lord for help. (2 Timothy 2: 22, GNT)

FIDELITY

He is committed to fidelity, Father.

This young man,
Newly-wed,
Said to me:
'Every day I ask God to keep me faithful to her,
To keep me always loving just her.'

He is handsome,
With a body toned by hours in the gym,
And a gentle manner—
A man attractive to women.
But he is honest about temptation,
And committed to fidelity
In a society in which infidelity is a national sport.
And so he asks you each day
To keep him faithful
To the one he has chosen
For life.

Help me to commit to fidelity, too, Father—
Faithful to the one I have chosen,
And faithful to you.

All those prayers are coming together now so you will do this well, fearless in your struggle, keeping a firm grip on your faith and on yourself. After all, this is a fight we're in. (1 Timothy 1: 18, MSG)

FAITH

Thank you for her faith, Father.

I think, sometimes, you brought us together
    to balance my faith.
She chides me when I want too much,
    and when I want to know too much.
She reminds me what it means to trust.
Her faith seems simpler than mine—
    yet more mature.
it seems my subconscious prayer is
    'Father, help me to understand.'
Her subconscious prayer is better:
    'Father, I do not need to understand;
    Help me to trust.'

Thank you for her faith, Father,
For through her faith
    you build mine.
Am I nurturing her faith, Father?

For I want very much to see you, in order to share a spiritual blessing with you to make you strong. What I mean is that both you and I will be helped at the same time, you by my faith and I by yours. (Romans 1: 11–12, GNT)

FAILED TO COMMUNICATE

We failed to communicate Father.

She said I didn't listen—
I never listen!
I said she didn't tell me—
She often thinks things
    and believes she has said them aloud!

It doesn't really matter who is right, Father.
We failed to listen,
    to words or to emotions;
We failed to understand;
We failed to support each other;
We simply competed for freedom from blame.

How often do we fail to communicate with you, Father?
We do not really listen.
We complain that you have not heeded us,
Because things have not happened
    the way we asked.
We are too busy telling you
    to really listen to you.

Forgive us, Father.
Help us to learn to communicate
    with one another,
And with you.

When I want to tell you about me,
Hush me,
So that I may learn about you.

Finally, brothers and sisters, rejoice! Strive for full restoration, encourage one another, be of one mind, live in peace. And the God of love and peace will be with you. (1 Corinthians 13: 11, NIV)

DOUBLE BED

Thank you for the double bed, Father.

We have argued,
    and now must share a bed.
Somehow the softness of our bodies
    softens the barrier between us.
The closeness brings us closer.
As we toss about,
We subconsciously touch each other—
    her leg draped across mine,
    my arm upon her waist,
    our hands joined…
Who can stay angry and distant
In a double bed?

Our children love the double bed.
It is the family comfort communication centre—
The place where
    upsets are soothed,
    bad dreams calmed,
    advice dispensed,
    movies shared,
    problems discussed,
    fears expressed,
    happiness passed on,
    love known …

You and I share a special place, too, Father.
A place where you hear
    my joys and troubles,
    my successes and struggles,
    my delights and concerns,
    my love and doubts,
    my confidence and inadequacies;
And where you remind me of
    your love,
    your compassion,
    your understanding,
    your care,
    your promises—
To humanity,
And to me.

Will it always be a place
Where we can be close?

Here's what I want you to do: Find a quiet, secluded place so you won't be tempted to role-play before God. Just be there as simply and honestly as you can manage. The focus will shift from you to God, and you will begin to sense his grace. (Matthew 6: 6, MSG)

LOVE THEIR MOTHER

My children need me to love their mother, Father.

I heard that
The best thing a man can do for his children
Is to love their mother.

I think it's true, Father.
If I love her,
If they know that I love her,
They will learn that conflict can be resolved
    without aggression, point-scoring or undermining.
They will learn that they are loved and valued,
    not treated as property to be fought over.
They will learn that women should be treated with respect,
    as partners, not minions.
They will learn that love
Sometimes struggles,
Sometimes hurts,
But seeks the best for the other,
Not the self.

I think, Father,
That my children need me to love you, too.
If I love you,
If they know that I love you,
They will learn that life is purposeful,
    not a pointless meandering towards death.

They will learn that in service for you is found
    ultimate freedom and fulfilment.
They will learn that they are accepted,
    loved unconditionally,
    no matter how people may judge them.
They will learn that there is joy to be found
    in putting others before ourselves.
They will learn the good news,
    that we win your favour not by our own efforts,
    but through your grace.
They will learn that your Spirit is always with us,
    within us,
    comforting, encouraging, challenging, guiding.

Is that what my children are learning, Father,
From me?

You are like light for the whole world. A city built on a hill cannot be hid. No one lights a lamp and puts it under a bowl; instead it is put on the lampstand, where it gives light for everyone in the house. In the same way your light must shine before people, so that they will see the good things you do and praise your Father in heaven. (Matthew 5: 14–16, GNT)

HOLDING TIGHT

She grasped my finger, Father,
Wrapped her tiny hand around it,
Her fingers barely reaching half way.
But she held on
    tightly,
        with a grip that belied her size.

It is ironic,
Because I am wrapped
    around *her* little finger.
She has captured me,
Shackled my heart to hers.

You too have captured me, Father.
Shackled my heart to yours.
Keep me holding on.

Hold on to what is good. (1 Thessalonians 5: 21, NIV)

ASKING

She asks a lot of me, Father.

I told her: 'You ask a lot of me.'
She knew it was not a complaint—
    just a flippant observation.
But her answer took me by surprise:
'I do, and you always answer me.'

I do?
I do.
Not because I must, but
    because I want to,
    because I love her,
And she knows it.

I learnt it from you, Father.
I ask a lot of you—
    every day,
And you always respond.
Thank you for your patient love.

If you remain in me and my words remain in you, then you will ask for anything you wish, and you shall have it. (John 15: 7, GNT)

JUMPING

She Jumped into my arms, Father.

She stood on the table
    and leapt into space at my call,
Knowing I would be there,
    trusting my arms to catch her,
    trusting my love to save her.

I remember when she became part of us,
    aged two:
Insecure;
Unable to walk properly;
Trusting nothing and no-one;
Fearful at being lifted up,
    or even lowered onto her back;
Terrified of any height.

But we taught her to trust our love.
Day by day,
Little by little,
She has learnt that we will not leave her,
    nor send her away.
She has learnt to trust our love.
Now she will leap from a table,
    trusting my arms.

Don't give up on me, Father.
I'm still learning to trust your love.

I'm still learning that you will always be there;
That I can step out in faith at your calling,
    and your arms will catch me.
Teach me to trust your love.

Yes, because GOD's your refuge, the High God your very own home, evil can't get close to you, harm can't get through the door. He ordered his angels to guard you wherever you go. If you stumble, they'll catch you; their job is to keep you from falling. (Psalm 91: 9–11, MSG)

ACROSS THE ROOM

He overflows with life and joy, Father.

In a new place,
It takes a few minutes for him to relax,
To feel comfortable with his surroundings,
    and these people;
But his energy cannot be suppressed.
Before long,
He is playing and laughing
With an exuberance that is irresistible.

But sometimes it overflows,
Overwhelming him,
Until he finds himself losing control.

We have an understanding.
Even across a room,
I need simply catch his eye,
And make a gesture—
Screwing the cap on the bottle
Before all the bubbles get out.

He smiles.
He understands.
He responds.

Am I ever like that with you, Father—
Living with an exuberance that is irresistible?

In Jesus,
You gave me life fulfilled,
    life abundant,
    life richer than I could have imagined.
Thank you, Father.
Help me
To let the bubbles out.

You provide delicious food for me in the presence of my enemies. You have welcomed me as your guest; blessings overflow! (Psalm 23: 5, TLB)

A MAN LIKE ME

What sort of man am I, Father?

The speaker explained how important Dads are
    in their children's lives.
When he said that
    my son will grow up to be
        remarkably like me,
I felt proud.
I will teach him to be a man.
But then he said
That my daughter—my vulnerable little princess—
    will probably bring home a man
        remarkably like me.
No!
I want better for her than that.

I'm confused.
What sort of hypocrite am I?
How can I want my son to be like me,
But not my daughter's partner?

Who am I—
    really?
What are the traits I want to see in my son
And in my daughter's partner?
What is it about me that I want to hide,
    not seen,
    not copied,

By impressionable children?

You know, don't you Father?
I know you love me as I am,
But you know who I can be,
And who I choose to be.

Will you teach me, Father,
    so that I raise my children right?
Will you examine me,
    and set me right?

LORD, you have examined me and you know me. You know everything I do; from far away you understand all my thoughts. (Psalm 139: 1–2, GNT)

PRAM

We were just looking for a pram, Father.

It seemed so simple.
What were we looking for?
A comfortable capsule,
    wheels,
      handle.
How hard could it be?

But no!
One has four wheels, another three;
One is for walking, another for jogging;
One fits in the car, another may not;
One protects from sun and wind;
One comes with a bag;
One has a drink holder;
One is a shopping trolley;
One has pneumatic tyres …
The list is endless.

And then there are colours.
Pink will be lovely for our angel—
    but what if we have a boy next?
White is neutral and fashionable—
    but will it get dirty?
Dark shades are 'serviceable'—
    but is serviceable what I want for this blossom?

Do you smile or frown as you watch me choose, Father?
Not just with prams,
> but in all the choices of my life.

Help me, Father, with choices.
Teach me to choose wisely,
And to teach my child to choose wisely.

Choose my instruction instead of silver, knowledge rather than choice gold. (Proverbs 8: 10, NIV)

PARENT

I'm a parent, Father.

I hold this little one—
Vulnerable, fragile, totally dependent on me
    to feed her,
    clothe her,
    protect her from all the things that can hurt her—
To love her.

Who am I?
What great skills or knowledge or wisdom do I have
    to presume to take on such a task?
Yet from me she will learn
    so many of her attitudes and value,
Including those I don't even know I'm teaching her.
Sometimes the responsibility overwhelms me.

Help me, Father.
    to be the parent she needs.
Help me to teach her about life.
Help me to teach her about love.
Help me to teach her about you.

So keep these commandments carefully in mind. Tie them to your hand to remind you to obey them, and tie them to your forehead between your eyes! Teach them to your children. Talk about them when you are sitting at home, when you are out walking, at bedtime, and before breakfast! (Deuteronomy 11: 18–20, TLB)

KISSES

She kissed me so gently, Father.

Holding my face in her hands
    as lightly as if I was a kitten;
She examined it,
    and then placed a kiss on the spot she had chosen.

We played a game:
When she kissed me,
    I pointed to another place on my face and said,
    'No, here';
And when she kissed that place,
    I pointed to another,
    then another,
    and another …
Until I was plastered in kisses.

Sometimes I think I demand too much of her love,
Yet she never complains.

Sometimes I think I demand too much of your love,
Father,
But I never hear you complain.
Thank you for loving me so much.

Praise the LORD. Give thanks to the LORD, for he is good; his love endures forever. (Psalm 106: 1, NIV)

MAN

I love to hold her, Father.

She is nestled, warm and snug, in my arms—
    my baby.
    my child,
    my precious.
I lack the words to articulate how I feel.

I carry scars of strife.
How can I hold such innocence?
How can I raise her right?
How can I show her how to live her life?

And yet—
    she does not judge or question,
    she vents no condemnation,
    she does not tell me that I'm not up to scratch.
Instead, she smiles at me.

So I can no longer be a boy,
    reckless,
    self-absorbed.
I will be a better man than I have ever been.
I will teach her what to expect of men
    and what a man should be.

I will teach her that
    stubble chin and heady sweat,
    deep voice and steely muscle,
    tattoos and hairy chest,
Are not the measures of a man—
But love,
And faith,
A willingness to sacrifice and serve,
    for love of her,
    for love of others,
    and for love of you, Father.

A good man brings good things out of the good stored up in his heart, and an evil man brings evil things out of the evil stored up in his heart. For the mouth speaks what the heart is full of. (Luke 6: 45, NIV)

FATHER FIGURE

I'm her father figure, Father.

She has no Dad in her life,
So I am to be the adult male for her.
But, Father, what do Dads do?
What did I do with my own children?
What will I teach her?
What will I be for her?

So here's my draft list, Father:
I will show her the unconditional love of a male—
    love that asks for nothing in return.
I will model how she should expect men to treat her—
    with respect, courtesy, unselfishness,
    putting her first in their affections and attentions.
I will show her that she has worth in herself—
    with no need to fit someone else's mould.
I will affirm her—
    to give her confidence in who she is.
I will show her that she is loved and loveable—
    not needing to compromise her values to receive
    love.
I will give her time—
    not just to do, but simply to be.
I will give her optimism and hope—
    the confidence that the world has a hopeful future.
And I will fix things—
    a broken doll or a broken heart.

I will set boundaries for her—
> boundaries that are reasonable and fair,
> but which teach her to be safe.

I will model for her the love of a partner
> in my relationship with my wife—
> to show her how men relate to women they love.

I will show her Jesus—
> so that she can learn to underpin her life with faith.

I will do stuff with her—
> to adventure, play, laugh and be a little silly.

And sometimes I will be quiet with her—
> to show that I enjoy her companionship.

What a list, Father—
> and I may think of more!

Am I up to it?
When I fail,
> step in,
> correct me,

And care for her.
Help her to be all that you created her to be.

I'm writing as a father to you, my children. I love you and want you to grow up well, not spoiled. There are a lot of people around who can't wait to tell you what you've done wrong, but there aren't many fathers willing to take the time and effort to help you grow up. (1 Corinthians 4: 14–15, MSG)

MISSING HIM

I'm missing him, Father.

In ways I can't understand
    I am grieving.
I've been away five days on business,
    and I'm missing him.

I understand missing my wife:
We talk on the phone;
I can picture her wherever she is;
We're accustomed to the occasional parting.

But with this baby—
I just want to hold him,
    to see his smile,
    to hear his gurgling chatter,
    to smell him,
    to plaster him with my kisses.

I want it so much it aches.
Like my memories of first love—
Whenever we were apart
    I could not erase her from my mind;
She infused all my thoughts.
It's that feeling all over again
    with this baby!

Do you feel like that with me, Father?
When I go away,
    even for a short time,
Do you yearn for my return,
Long to hear me talking to you again?

You, like your ancestors before you, have turned away from my laws and have not kept them. Turn back to me, and I will turn to you. (Malachi 3: 7, GNT)

INTERESTS

I never know what will interest my kids, Father.

Ellie sees a brief excerpt from a ballet
    and spends the next fifteen years learning dance.
Jeremy sees gymnastics at the local hall
    and that's what he determines to do.
Jenny sees someone playing a flute,
    and commits to excelling as a flautist.

I cannot know what will appeal to them,
    nor why.
Sometimes I nudge them
    into the path of choices I think will appeal
    and enable them to thrive.
But I can only guide their choices,
By exposing them to appropriate experiences,
    reliable role models,
    trusted mentors,
And talking through with them
    the choices they make.

Is that how you feel about me, Father?
Do I surprise you with the choices I make?
Do you sometimes nudge me into the path of right choices?

It's in Christ that we find out who we are and what we are living for. (Ephesians 1: 11, MSG)

STARING

I caught her staring again, Father.

I look down at her,
Only to find her staring up at me.
It fascinates me.
Is it love?
Is it discovery?
Is it searching to understand me?

All I know is that it delights me
That she wants to explore my face
And understand my mind,
    and my heart.

I don't think I do that enough with you, Father.
I should spend more time staring into your face—
Seeking to know you better,
Seeking to search what is in your heart.
Forgive me for not staring enough.

Glory in his holy name; let the hearts of those who seek the LORD rejoice. Look to the LORD and his strength; seek his face always. Psalm 105: 3–4, NIV)

WITH YOU

'I just want to be with you.'
That's what he said, Father.

I was busy doing what I thought important,
Shut away in my room.
And then unannounced, unexpected,
He was there beside me,
Squatting on the floor,
Running the toy car across the carpet.

'Why are you here?' I asked,
Resentful at the intrusion
    into my space,
    into my thoughts;
And he simply said,
'I just want to be with you.'

Guilt. That was my first feeling.
Tenderness, my second.
What did I do to be so blessed?
What did I do to deserve such love?
What did I do that he should want nothing more
    than to be with me—
Not expecting a story nor a game;
Just wanting to be with me.

Is that how you feel, Father?
I ask so much:
    do this for me,
    help that person,
    solve this problem,
    make that happen.
You must think me a demanding child.
How delighted you must be
    when I just want to be in your presence.

So here I am, Father—
    no agenda,
    no requests,
Just wanting to be with you.

Seek the Lord while he may be found; call on him while he is near. (Isaiah 55: 6, NIV)

HIS HERO

I'm his hero, Father.

I never thought of myself worthy to be anyone's hero,
    but I am to him.
Because I fixed his toy,
    he thinks I can fix anything.
Because I carried him,
    he thinks I am strong enough to carry anything.
Because I know answers to his questions,
    he thinks I know everything.
Because …
    he thinks I can …

And I'm sometimes afraid:
Afraid that there will come a time when
    I will fail him, let him down,
        unable to solve his problem,
        or to meet his need.
What then?
When he sees my weakness, will I have failed?

Or do I simply need to teach him
That when I am no longer able,
You are able?

You, LORD, give perfect peace to those who keep their purpose firm and put their trust in you. (Isaiah 26: 3, GNT)

TIME

They just want time, Father.

'Quality time' is a myth,
    used to justify limited time.
But they just want time:
To join Dad on a trip to the hardware store;
To join Mum shopping for clothes;
To help cook the meal;
To lift and carry and sort out the shed;
To walk, throw a frisbee, kick a ball;
To tidy the toys, or play with them—
    together.
Doing anything, but doing it
    together,
Before they decide that
    we don't really want their company,
    so they can do without ours.

I enjoy your company, Father—
Just talking,
Not about anything intense,
Just about you, and me, and us and life.
Thank you for being a Father
    who always has time.

Seek the Lord while you can find him. Call upon him now while he is near. (Isaiah 55: 6, TLB)

THANKS

I'm glad to be a Dad and a Poppa, Father.

Thank you for the children with whom you've blessed my life—
For their arms which cling to me and give me strength to do;
For their playfulness;
For the joy and healing they bring with their laughter;
For their excitement in achieving new things;
For the tears I shed as I watch them grow;
For their boisterousness and energy;
For their delight in giving gifts;
For their wonder in learning new things;
For the simple truths they share with me;
And the unconditional love they show.

Thank you for Jesus,
Who knew you as Father,
And taught us to know you as Father too.
Teach me to love as you, my Father, have loved—
    unconditionally,
        extravagantly.

Jesus said to them, 'When you pray, say this: "Father: ... "'
(Luke 11: 2, GNT)

Also by Phil Ridden:

Reflections on faith inspired by Children

Reflections on faith inspired by Seniors

Reflections on faith inspired by Babies

Reflections on faith inspired by COVID

Faith around the barbecue (The story)

Faith around the barbecue (The play)

www.philridden.com.au

www.ingramcontent.com/pod-product-compliance
Lightning Source LLC
Chambersburg PA
CBHW070434010526